Sun

Look for the other books on weather by

Marion Dane Bauer
Rain • Wind • Clouds
Snow • Rainbow

SIMON SPOTLIGHT

An imprint of Simon & Schuster Children's Publishing Division

1230 Avenue of the Americas, New York, New York 10020

This Simon Spotlight edition May 2016

Text copyright © 2016 by Marion Dane Bauer

Illustrations copyright © 2016 by John Wallace

For information about special discounts for bulk purchases, please contact Simon & Schuster
Special Sales at 1-866-506-1949 or business@simonandschuster.com.

Manufactured in the United States of America 0416 LAK

2 4 6 8 10 9 7 5 3 1

Library of Congress Cataloging-in-Publication Data

Names: Bauer, Marion Dane, author. | Wallace, John, 1966- illustrator.

Title: Sun / by Marion Dane Bauer ; illustrated by John Wallace.

Description: New York : Simon Spotlight, [2016] | Series: Ready-to-read

Identifiers: LCCN 2015046176 | ISBN 9781481463393 (pbk.) | ISBN 9781481463409
(hardcover)

Subjects: LCSH: Sun—Juvenile literature.

Classification: LCC QB521.5 .B38 2016 | DDC 523.7—dc23

LC record available at http://lccn.loc.gov/2015046176

ISBN 9781481463416 (eBook)

Sun

written by Marion Dane Bauer
illustrated by John Wallace

Ready-to-Read

Simon Spotlight
New York   London   Toronto   Sydney   New Delhi

Did you know
that every morning
you are wakened by a star?

The same star gives you
light all day long.

It warms you too.

This star is called
the Sun.

Our Sun is just one
of more than
100 billion stars
in the Milky Way,
our galaxy.

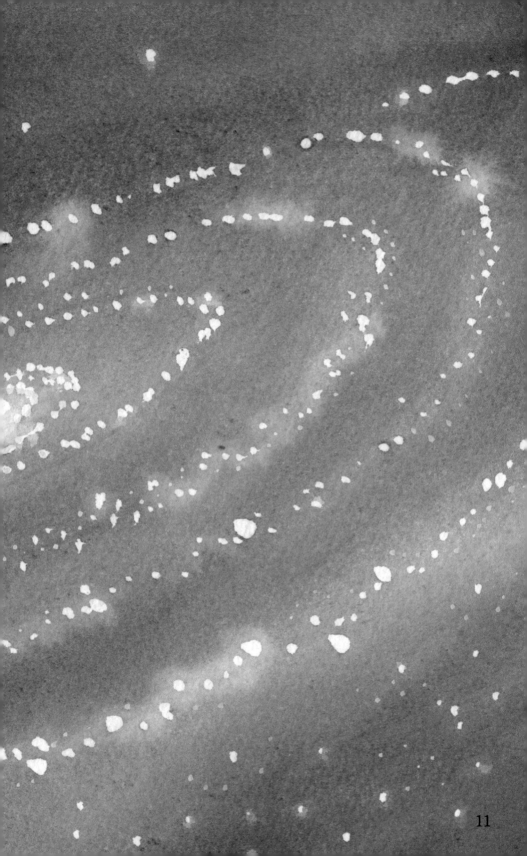

Many, many more stars exist
beyond our galaxy too,
more than anyone can
count or even see.

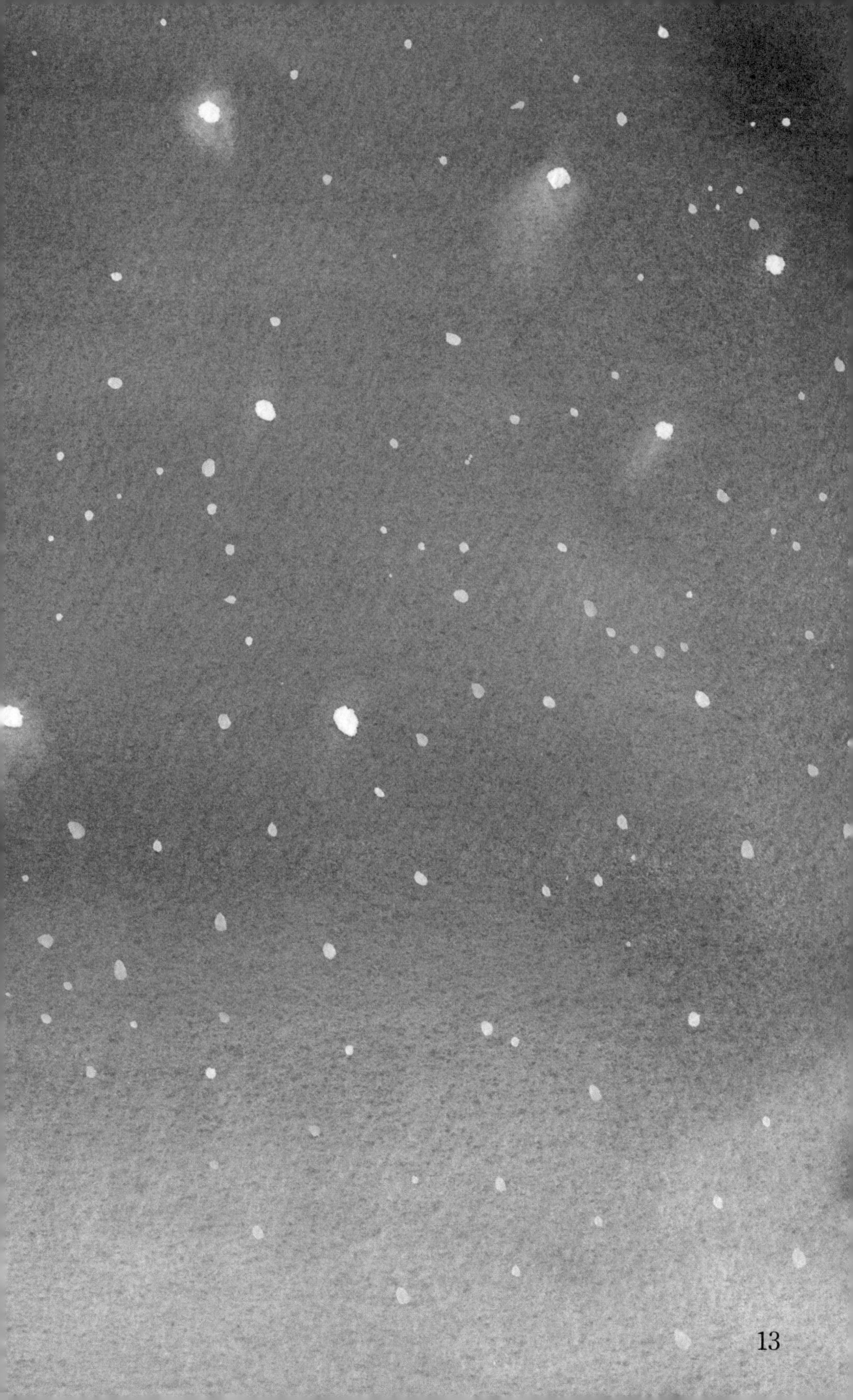

Our Sun is not the
biggest of all the stars.

It is not the hottest,
either.

But it is the one
that is closest to us.
That is why it looks
so big.

That is also why
it is so important to us!

Of all the planets circling
our Sun, Earth is the
lucky one.

It is just the right
distance from the Sun.

If we were too close,
our water would turn
to steam and disappear
into the air.

If we were too far away,
our water would all be ice.

Life needs water.

Bacteria and elephants,
plants and birds,
bugs and us . . .

. . . we all need water.

We need light and warmth, too.
And we need vitamin D
from the Sun
to make our bones strong.

We need the Sun.

Thank you, Sun!

Facts about the Sun:

- The Sun is about 93 million miles from Earth.

- The next closest star is 250 thousand times farther away.

- The Sun is more than 100 times bigger than Earth.

- Our Earth rotates around the Sun. It takes 365.25 days—one year—to go around once. That is why we have leap years, to gather up those quarter days and keep the calendar on track.

- The Sun is made of burning gases.

- Imagine how hot you feel on a summer day when the temperature reaches 100 degrees Fahrenheit. The surface of the Sun is about 10,000 degrees Fahrenheit. The center of the Sun is even hotter, about 27 million degrees Fahrenheit.

- Our Sun is a middle-aged star, 4.5 billion years old. In another 5 billion years it will begin to die. But we won't be here then to see the change. Even our great-great-great-grandchildren will no longer be here.

- Because Earth tilts, the angle of the sunlight changes. The changing angle of the sunlight— sometimes high, sometimes low—gives us our changing seasons.